All Scripture references taken from the KJV of the Holy Bible.

Do Not Swear by the Moon: Triangular Powers

Dr. Marlene Miles

Freshwater Press, USA

ISBN: 978-1-960150-41-7

Copyright 2023 by Dr. Marlene Miles

All rights reserved. No part of this book may be reproduced, distributed, or transmitted by any means or in any means including photocopying, recording or other electronic or mechanical methods without prior written permission of the publisher except in the case of brief publications or critical reviews.

Table of Contents

Introduction 5

God's In His Heaven 8

The Moon *god* 11

Pray for Another Day 17

We Do Not Worship the Moon 20

What Is the Moon Really Doing? 22

The Cool Enemy 25

Temple Idols 28

Parents Pay, Children Pay 31

Deliverance from the Moon *god* 34

Uncommon Failure 37

Raise Your Child 40

They Are Serious, Aren't You? 42

The Take Over 45

The Saved Life 50

I'm Not Enchanted to Meet You 53

Warrior Angels 57

The Four One-One 64

For Our Words 66

Warfare & Deliverance Prayers 68

Prayerbooks by this author 88

Other books by this author 89

Do Not Swear by the Moon
Triangular Powers

But I tell you not to swear at all, either by heaven or it is God's thrown, or by the earth, for it is his footstool, or by Jerusalem, for this the city of the Great King. (Matthew 5:33-34).

Freshwater

Introduction

The previous book in this *Triangular Powers* series was **SUNBLOCK,** it was about the sun. This book, **Do Not Swear by the Moon** is Book 3 in the series.

When it comes to swearing, don't; all you need to say is a simple yes or no. Otherwise you will be condemned, the Word says.

Above all my brothers, do not swear, not by heaven, nor by Earth, nor by anything else.

(James 5:12)

We will talk about two kinds of evil connected to the moon. Those who align themselves with the moon, knowingly and those who do it unknowingly. Either, or both of these types of people could be affecting my life, your life, the life of the people you know, your community, even your whole country.

There are warfare prayers at the end of this book for a mighty Deliverance.

Let's contrast the Powers Above, to the ***powers*** of Ephesians 6: *Rulers, principalities, spiritual wickedness--*, the entities in the 2nd heaven. *Triangular Powers are* the major God-created celestial bodies, the sun, moon, and stars.

As you are reading this book, you may have read the first two books of this series: **Powers Above** and **SUNBLOCK**. The 4th book of the series is entitled, **Starstruck**.

Reviewing, God made the entire universe and all the elements in the heavens. He made the heavens to declare His glory. God lives in the 3rd Heaven. But there is evil still under the sun, because the hearts of men are wicked, and the devil is wicked.

For we wrestle not against flesh and blood, but against principalities, against powers, against the rulers of the darkness of this world, against spiritual wickedness in high places. (Ephesians 6:12)

Satan is in the 2nd Heaven, <u>confirming</u> that there *is* spiritual wickedness in high places.

God's In His Heaven

God's in His heaven—
All's right with the world!

Robert Browning

God, in Genesis created everything, including the heavens and the heavenly powers: the sun, the moon, the stars, three powerful lights that govern the Earth. These mighty elements can affect humans positively or negatively. The sun rules the day. The moon, which is the lesser light compared to the sun, stands guard over the night. They are different, but everything God has made is awesome.

Humans are also awesome because God made us. In our authority and proper Godly positions, we can command the sun, the moon, the Earth, and all the works of His hand. God made us a little lower than Elohim and put us in authority over much. God is in His Heaven and man is set to rule in Earth; as long as order is maintained, all will be right with the world.

By day, we live our lives joyously by the bounteous light of the sun. By night, the dimmer light of the moon may make us behave differently if we are sight-walkers instead of those who walk by faith. Something happens to mankind at night. Is it because of the darkness or the lesser light of the lesser element, the moon? If we believe the moon can speak, then we will believe what the moon tells us in its dim, romantic, or spooky light.

Abiding by only moonlight and nothing greater or brighter, well --, that is good as sin and Satan want it. Both sin and Satan love the night because if people would walk only by the light of the moon instead of the light of the sun, then Satan can better carry out his plans. He can better run his game against people.

In the night-time, sin talks folks into all kinds of stuff.

Without the Light of the Son, Jesus Christ, any of us could believe many wrong things at many wrong times. The Light of the World which is far greater than the light of the sun reveals

Truth, while the moon keeps things hidden. It keeps secrets such as sin and the *occult*. There are a lot of secret societies and clubs, which we will discuss in this book.

The devil has convinced a lot of people that he doesn't even exist. Sadly, some who know that the devil exists may also have been convinced that the devil is as powerful as God. That's not true; he's not, but the devil does use a lot of tricks and distraction to parlay his game against mankind.

The Moon *god*

Under the light of the moon there are many tricks and distractions. That little light that shines dimly most of the time, and brightly, infrequently can't do what the sun does, but She tries. A lot of people believe the moon and they believe *in* the moon. Some believe there is a man in the moon, others serve the *gods* and *goddesses* associated with the moon. Some don't even realize that they are serving those *gods*.

If the moon's, little g *god*, is in your ancestral foundation, in your generational bloodline, then oaths and vows have been made to this *little g **god***, giving it <u>lifetime</u> and bloodline rights to your family into the 3rd, 4th, I don't know, maybe to the 5th generation and beyond. Pledges of loyalty unto death may have been made if alliances have been formed with the little g *god* that is associated with the moon.

The only way out of this bloodline pledge is to renounce it and repent to God. Renounce it and uproot the cause of the curse completely. Pray that God forgives. Amen.

God made mankind to be set in Dominion, to have dominion over the Earth, and to have dominion over all of the works of God's creation. But, when you or anyone in your bloodline makes vows and evil oaths, they give their power and authority over to Satan. A person might do this because of false promises of *things, stuff,* position, power, or fame from the devil. But when a human gives up their authority and position in God, they become victims of the devil, themselves.

Oaths to idol *gods* is sin, idolatry is sin. Every *little g god* is an alter ego or a version of the devil or you can say these entities work for the devil. The pledge or oath is made, there's the sin, and there's the devil. Once the devil is in anything there will be at least one curse in the life of the sinner.

Once the devil gets in a bloodline the entire bloodline falls victim to that same curse. We must say, victims--, because there will be multiple and generational victims of even one evil oath, vow, covenant, or curse. **Time** enters to make that curse last forever, if the devil has his way against the sinner.

Once Adam & Eve had sinned, the devil was ready to attach a forever clock to enforce the curse against an entire bloodline. That's like a man buying a car from the devil, owing for the car, paying all his life for that car, but when he dies the loan starts all over again for the same car and now his son has to pay for that old, raggedy car that he doesn't even want. Then the son dies, and *his* son has to pay for a car that doesn't even run anymore. The counterfeit promises of the devil may be up on blocks, but the grandson is still paying for it.

The car maybe towed to the junkyard and never seen by the great grandson who is still paying for a *"car"* that he knows nothing about, and has never seen, but he is wondering why his life is going so badly and why his money is being drained away from him.

That's what sin does.

God on the other hand is a forgiving Father, who if you repent and ask forgiveness, He will forgive you and restore right order. Back in our proper positions where God has given us authority and set us in dominion, we have authority over all of the works of God's hands--, even cars--, if we make the right decisions, walk upright before the Lord and don't make evil, devil-deals.

A man could sin day or night, but there is something enticing about the night that that can induce a man to sin. It's that mysterious moon in all its presentations.

Sin demotes a man, changing God's order, diminishing, or completely usurping a man's spiritual authority. Sin demotes a man so severely that now other curses can alight on that man – curses sent by the devil through evil human agents in the Earth.

Recapping, this book is about those who serve the idol *gods* of the moon knowingly and unknowingly. **Evil human agents** who knowingly serve the devil for whatever reasons can send curses to unsuspecting others via the moon. Those curses can alight because those "others" have unrepented sin in their lives, whether idolatry or other sins. Sin is sin.

If we don't violate the order of God, we can command these evil demons, devils and powers and curses will not alight on us. We do this by commanding the day, every day. If we don't, evil entities and evil human agents will. And they'll even use God's creation *against* us. We should command the night for the same reason. In our prayers at the back of this book, we do both--, full force.

Man has evil in his heart, and man has devised a way to use, to *triangulate* the power and the **Triangular Powers** against other men in the Earth. Evil is full rebellion and will corrupt or abuse anything. Abusing these celestial powers is almost second nature to people who have been born into or indoctrinated into the lifestyle early in their lives.

Abuse of these **Triangular Powers** could be why your prayers don't seem to be answered by God. It could be why your deliverance is delayed or hindered, or why your life really needs to be going better--, *Triangular Powers* could be working against you.

Easy stuff is hard for you. There are ridiculous setbacks in your life and possibly worse. If that is so, you can suspect ***Triangular Powers*** at work.

Triangular Powers do not themselves decide to affect your life negatively. The elements were created to glorify God, and to be a blessing to mankind. Whomever is **working** evil in the Earth either against you or any evil that *affects* you may be using *Triangular Powers*. This can powerfully, and stubbornly affect the course of what should be your abundant life.

Is your life abundant? Jesus came that you might have life, abundantly. If you don't have the things that Jesus said you should have and you are one of His, and you live a prayerful and fasted life – suspect *Triangular Powers* are in operation against you.

Pray for Another Day

Curses and evil covenants will get you coming and going. First, you shouldn't make an evil covenant. You should not swear a vow or make a blood oath to anything that has nothing to do with God. Being in the ungodly covenant is bad enough, it's terrible actually – but when you go to break it other troubles may erupt; that's how being in the covenant will get you coming and *going*.

When you go to break covenant, if you don't do that properly with a godly prayer covering, the enemy you were once aligned with, will now be coming after you because even the devil has the nerve to complain of broken covenant.

Above all, my brothers, do not swear. No do not swear, not by heavens or by earth or anything else. All you need to say is a simple yes or no, otherwise you'll be condemned. (James 5:12)

You should pray, whether you *think* you need it or not. Pray. Prayers transcend space and time. The prayer or prayers that you pray that you may think you don't even need--, maybe you don't need it, right then, but those prayers will be waiting for you in your future when you get there, or maybe when your child has a need, the prayer is there. Prayed already. That prayer, especially a prayer of repentance, may keep your grandson or great grandson from **paying** for a *car* that doesn't exist anymore.

Grandma's prayers, mama's prayers—especially prayers of protection, and for Wisdom--, those prayers have covered you like a heavy quilt in the cold of winter, like a weighted blanket. Heavy covering. Thank you, Mama, Thank you Grandma/Grandpa. Thank You, Lord.

If you're walking upright before God and you've prayed everything you think you can pray, everything you can find to pray about, and you're asking, *Where is your deliverance? Where is your reward? Where's your peace? Where's your victory?* Have you prayed against **Triangular**

Powers and the abuse of them? Then, do it and watch your situation change for your good.

We Do Not Worship the Moon

We do not worship the moon. We do not worship any of the *Triangular Powers*. We do not worship the sun or the stars. We don't worship Angels. We don't worship people or things. We only worship God. Amen.

The sun is **not** a God. Jehovah God does not live in the sun. The moon is not a *god* but there is a little g *god* that is associated with the moon and some other entities from ancient mythology (Greek, Roman, Egyptian, Norse, Celtic, et cetera) that are associated with the moon. We are not polytheistic, and we do not worship <u>**any**</u> of these idol *gods*.

The moon is supposed to be working for us, not against us, to affect Earth's atmosphere to make the planet more livable. The moon affects the oceans, lakes, and the larger bodies of water causing high and low tides. The sun has some effect on that too, but the moon is much closer to Earth, so it has more effect on tides and tidal waves than the sun.

The lunar cycle has impact on human reproduction, fertility, monthly cycles of women and birth rate. Melatonin levels appear to be correlated with menstrual cycles.

The moon also affects the migration and navigation of birds. That was a brief snapshot of what the moon is *supposed* to be doing in the natural for us.

God made the moon to serve man and to glorify God.

The heavens declare the glory of God, and the firmament showeth his handiwork.
(Psalm 19:1).

What Is the Moon Really Doing?

If we invoke the name of an entity or power to assist us in something we want to do or cause to happen, if that person or power is not God, if that name we're invoking is not the Name of Jesus, or His Holy Spirit, just because we are in the Earth, where the devil is the prince of the powers of the air, the devil or his representative will show up. The devil's goal is to get into or make covenant or alliance with a human, or to create a soul tie, because he can.

Unholy alliances are formed when we do something that we've decided or have been told is okay--, but it's not. For example, when we celebrate Halloween along with the evil people who *really* celebrate Halloween--, witches,

Wizards, warlocks, an unholy alliance is made. Sadly, annually that alliance is re-upped or renewed.

STOP agreeing with evil!

When you participate in Halloween or any version of that, you are agreeing with the highest day of Satan in the year. *Why*? Don't your children get candy all year?

Aside from the razor blades and all other evil *in* the candy, *enchantments* may have been pronounced **over** the candy that your child is bringing home and eating.

Dressing up for Halloween, carved pumpkin at the door--, do you not realize this initiates your child into Satan's camp? And it also indicates to the devil that they can take your youngest. Yeah, look that up for yourself if you don't believe me.

Why would we add our God-given grace to *that*?

When Christians are celebrating the resurrection of Jesus Christ, how many satanists do you think will join in that Holy Day?

You have to discern *spirits* to see who and what it is you're agreeing with, and what you are saying yes to. Always, always.

Their sorrows shall be
multiplied *that* hasten *after* another *god*: their
drink offerings of blood will I not offer, nor take
up their names into my lips. (Psalms 16:4)

The Cool Enemy

The moon is s a subtle enemy. A person who's cool and calculating like the moon can be very nice on the surface, cool and calm, but extremely dangerous. With that kind of an enemy, we all need serious prayer coverage.

Not to be Captain Obvious here, if you worship something, if you think that something is powerful, if you think it's a *deity*, you will eventually ask that something you worship to do something for you. When you do that's when the evil covenant is made. Next, it travels into bloodlines. People pass on these dark arts from generation to generation in families. Evil people trick the young, the ignorant, the innocent and try to recruit them into occultic initiations. Halloween is one such time. A lot of other pagan *gods* get **worship** in pagan holidays and festivals from unsuspecting people who most often do not give it a second thought. Halloween might be the most dangerous for all people, especially children.

God needs Christians to **agree** with *Him*, so godly things can happen in the Earth. God needs us to agree with the 3rd Heaven. But your TV, for instance, may be broadcasting 2nd heaven stuff 24 hours a day; and we watch it whether we mean to or not. We watch it, whether we want to or not. After a while we could get tripped up and tricked as we normalize what we see when 2nd heaven "stuff" should never become *normal* for a Christian.

Second heaven is Satanic headquarters, where there are all kinds of wicked and evil *spirits*, dangerous and fallen angels. Fallen angels have no love and no mercy for mankind, and we should never make any type of alliance or covenant with them. We should not have interaction with them. They are outlaws to God. Getting into cahoots with them is like harboring criminal fugitives in your home and trying to hide them from the cops.

This book is about moon worshippers. Yeah, there are moon worshippers. The name for the *God* in Islam was originally the name of the deity that lives in the moon, *Allah*. There are a bunch of little g *gods* and *goddesses* associated with the moon that were worshipped by Romans, Greeks, and Egyptians. These idol *gods* have found ways, century after century of garnering worship from suspecting and unsuspecting souls, some of these humans do not even know they've been *initiated*. How is that a big deal? Worshipping these idols, gives them power, and it gives them license to **live** in your life. If allowed, they will take over your life.

The moon *goddess*, Diana of Roman mythology was called Artemis by the Greeks. She goes by other names. Know that worship of idol *gods* is an affront to God, and a danger to your life now, and your eternal destination.

Furthermore, idolatry invites the devil in. We need to be sure that we are not even **accidentally** worshipping a false *god*.

Temple Idols

They didn't just worship these idol *gods*, they built whole temples for them. You don't build a house for a person unless you're serious about the relationship and are planning that they stay.

So that not only this our craft is in danger to be set at not, but also the temple of the great goddess Diana should be despised in her magnificence should be destroyed, whom all Asia and the world worship.

Acts 19:27

Diana was widely worshipped and that was a problem that can be seen all the way into the Book of the Revelations. People made little silver statues of Diana. Obviously, the people who are making money off of making idols, didn't want to tear down the temple or stop serving this idol *god* because that was their source of income.

But God had another plan in Ephesus, that busy center full of idolatry. God hates idolatry. Ephesus is in modern day Turkey and is now called Selcuk. The Temple of Artemis was built in that major city, which meant that people could easily come and buy the idols and they were easily exported to other cities.

In spite of that, Ephesus played a very strong part in **Christianity**. Paul went there and had a revival. He preached for 30 days, and many people were converted to Christianity.

On his third missionary trip, Apostle Paul held a two-year revival in Ephesus, where the people believed that the statue of Diana had fallen from the planet Jupiter and had landed in their midst, on the West Coast of Turkey--, and it didn't even break, it didn't shatter, didn't crumble, crack or bend when it hit the ground. They didn't know much about the Earth's atmosphere then, but we can be amazed that the massive statue didn't burn up when entering Earth. *Isn't that amazing?*

For all we know, they probably thought it landed upright and settled in their city.

We have a real and wicked enemy, who has evil human agents in the Earth. Folks, if we don't watch and pray, if we don't stay prayed up, we could get caught off guard. You are looking at visions 2 versus two and three, Wherein in time past ye walked according to the course of this world, according to the prince of the power of the air, the spirit that now worketh in the children of disobedience, (Ephesians 2:2)

In our times this *moon goddess* worship gets repackaged—again. Idols keep getting repackaged century after century; the devil is a master of advertising and marketing. From generation to generation moon, moon *god,* and moon *goddess* worship has been repackaged as Islam, Freemasons, Eastern Star, Shriners, and any number of college fraternities and sororities. All of those participating in these groups, give worship, knowingly or unknowingly to the *moon god,* Allah.

When oaths are secret, you pretty much know it's not only not of God, but also Satanic.

Parents Pay, Children Pay

Speaking of higher education, how many parents think that when they send their child off to college that they will begin *idol* worship? Some parents are super proud if their child pledges to a Greek fraternity or sorority. Perhaps parents don't know of about the secret oaths, secret missions, and hazing.

Perhaps the parents *do* know and these are legacy pledges, and they are really proud never having known or considered that this is a hidden way to recruit a person into idol *god* worship. Maybe the whole family is celebrating because this idol worship is in the bloodline already, but they just want their child to follow in their Alpha-Phi-*Whatever* footsteps. Those legacy parents have either given no thought to it, but they think that they can mesh this together with Christianity.

They can't serve more than Jehovah God, all else is idolatry.

Those who were oblivious to how their child's college education could negatively affect their Christianity you might want to reconsider. Christian parents, you have Christened your child, baptized your child, brought them up in the fear and admonition of the Lord, and now paying $20,000 a year for them to go to college and *lose* their Christian walk, or have it abased? Really?

Listen, after they start serving at strange altars of idol *gods* all the other sins that co-eds do in college is a cinch. But seriously, when did you turn *Greek*? Greeks are not trying to be Black or anything other than *Greek*.

The moment they pledge and swear oaths to idol *gods*, your child is captured!

And you **PAID** for that to happen.

Every frat house, every sorority house has at least one idol *god* associated with it. It could explain why your child's behavior is debased and gets raunchy after pledging Greek. ***Idol worship.***

Let's be reminded of Moses on Mount Sinai, the newly freed Israelites wandering in the wilderness–. Your child, newly freed, just got away from home, now wandering around on a college campus. The Israelites were at the foot of the mountain building idols and having orgies. What's your child doing now that they are "free" from your rules at home and their new *idol god* is telling them it's okay to "be free" and do the grownup all they want?

Dues paid to the fraternity is a form of idol worship. The group continues to get together long after college in the name of lasting friendship, brotherhood or sisterhood, but they really are renewing the ungodly covenant.

College fraternities and sororities are the training ground for Freemasons, Eastern Star and other secret societies.

Freemasons, Eastern Star, and Shriners get together far more often than annually or biannually – renewing the covenant.

These are some of the ways that even Americans are tied to this *moon god*, by both willing, and/or oblivious, and duped participants.

Deliverance from the Moon *god*

Deliverance prayers need to be prayed to be free from the *moon god (goddess)* – BUT! - deliverance will be hindered if you or your bloodline is **connected** to the moon *god,* or any *little g god* connected to any of the *Triangular Powers*. See the compromise here?

This could be a checkmate.

But God! God has another plan. The battleground is in the heavenlies. It is not at your house between you and your spouse. It is not at your workplace amongst co-workers, it is not on the church pew--, necessarily. We wrestle not against flesh and blood. So we take the fight to the proper arena--, in the heavenlies, and we have to defend ourselves, accordingly against Satanic attack. In prayer.

In the church--, no pew wars. We are not to be fighting with people in church. Of course, as you are discerning every *spirit*, let the Holy Ghost advise you because every "saint" --, ain't. People are on assignment against the Word, the people of God, and especially the pastor--, and LORD! The first lady--, I was one of those, I know about **first-lady warfare** that must be endured, *with a smile.*

The moon is not evil, nor was it created for evil, but it can be programmed with evil. To the negative, when it is programmed with evil, it can smite, it can burn, using the power of the moon. It can rule, not just over the night, but it could rule over people, over the Earth, as can the sun. The moon affects the oceans, the nations, it affects the whole Earth. This is serious; the moon is not cheese. Sorry, Wisconsin.

Because of the widespread effect of the moon, when incantations are sent to it and it's programmed with evil, it can program sickness into people, and occultic evil can be done against mankind. *Occultic* means– hidden, secret, so folks don't even see it coming.

Marriages, children, family, destinies, and wealth--, the things that make life good, and worthwhile can be blocked or hijacked. Christians are not occultic, they are at church just a *prayin''* out loud. *Monitoring spirits* are there in people or like that fly on the wall, reporting exactly what you're praying to God for and devising strategies to stop it.

The first attack is to compromise you by sin. Sin, which is Christian kryptonite, defiles and weakens you. It weakens you spiritually so now the devil can play with you like Play Doh.

Duh. Didn't you know that already, though?

Uncommon Failure

Sin leads to disaster. It can project poverty, loss, backwardness, among other things. I ask again, have you ever noticed things happening to you that's not really happening to everybody else? Easy things are hard for you, for no apparent reason. It is called *Uncommon failure*. Anyone in a dry, prayerless season is very susceptible to it.

You have to always stay prayed up because there are human agents abusing the *Triangular Powers--, the* moon, the full moon, especially, the Blue Moon. Strawberry Moons, Blood Moons, Pink Moons, Harvest Moon, Libra Moon.... They know all the moons. They study the moons. They are serious about this.

Occultic people use *Triangular Powers above* to keep people away from God, to keep people confused and living random, useless, purposeless lives. Confirming this: there are 500 million agnostics and atheists in the world, who need to hear the Word of God, the Gospel of Jesus Christ.

In no way does this mean that these atheists have NEVER heard the Word of God, they just have never heard the Word to the point that it gets into their hearts… their ears- to-hear are not open or there are other distractions keeping them from *really hearing* the Word. Sometimes it's external stimuli, other times its internal.

For example if a person worships money, the thought of joining the Body of Christ and paying tithes or giving offerings is offensive and off putting to them. They will run from God if they are already worshipping money. That's internal – nobody is *making* a person worship Mammon, it is either their own choice, or it may be in their family bloodline.

Jeremiah says, *As for me and my house we will serve the Lord.* There may have been a patriarch in your bloodline who said, as for him and his house, they would serve Mammon. They may not have used those exact words, but that was the covenant that was made for that man and his succeeding generations, unless someone, by the power of Christ, broke that evil covenant.

When those who practice evil use the *Triangular Powers*, it's to set up failures against breakthroughs for the Believer. Not just the Believer – those who practice the dark arts do not only hate Believers, but they also hate whomever else they choose--, usually whomever is not giving them what they want or doing as they wish.

Raise Your Child

      Again I warn, if your child is showing interest in magic of any kind, especially involving the sun, moon, or the stars, you need to teach your children God's way, not the way of evil. You need to teach them at all times.

      Delving into witchcraft or the Black Arts, Harry Potter, Ouija Boards, and the like, puts an invisible mark on a person. They will not only be attracted to more of that, but that mark will *attract* more evil and more evil dark arts workers to them.

      Perhaps you need deliverance because you or your spouse transferred something to your child at birth which made them evil-curious. You can't just blame your spouse and declare they need deliverance because you are married to him/her and you are *one*. Therefore you **both** need deliverance. Actually the whole family needs to submit to the Word and prayer, counseling and deliverance. Nip this in the bud so you don't have a household witch growing right there in your midst. You do not want to be feeding, clothing, and housing a *witch*.

NO! Don't kick your minor child out of the house, submit to deliverance.

Some families are afraid to pieces that their child will get introduced into crime or gang behavior. Hello, suburbanites and others, are you looking out to make sure your child is not being *jumped* into a coven?

Stay prayed up.

They Are Serious, Aren't You?

People who use *Triangular Powers* are very serious. They are not playing about the evil they want to accomplish. But hear this! They don't think there's anything *evil* about what they are doing. They don't think it's evil at all. They think it's justified – they feel that they've been wronged or offended and are doing what they think they have a right to do. Many of these people are ALSO going to church and believed they are SAVED. I saw an ad last year for a "Christian witches conference!" That cannot exist, God hates the practice of witchcraft.

My GOD of Mercy!

Nowadays, idolatry is repackaged real pretty too. Every generation or so it can get a makeover so the young people who don't listen to their parents or elders will believe they are doing something "new," when there is nothing new under the sun. In this way, people accept it all over again, thinking it's new, better, or more powerful.

People who call themselves *spirit guides*, or say they have spirit guides, are listening to *familiar spirits* and *guardian demons*. People who say they are *light workers, star children,* all other kinds of *new ageism*, and witchy words are not of God, not from God, not by God. They are not for you. They are not Christian. They are not godly; they're not trying to help you.

Yeah, the satanic agents are trying to get power and get paid. If you buy into what they're selling, you end up aligning yourself with the evil of The Dark World and the dark arts, the dark powers. They may be totally deceived and think they are working in the *light*, and they're working for good--, not so. They are not working for God only God is Good and Jesus is the Light of the World.

Not to linger here, but I've seen deceived so-called "light workers" make social media videos and put Christian music as their background sound. They could have a Bible nearby. It's a prop. These types are all over Christian sites commenting, arguing--, disliking mostly.

We have to discern every *spirit,* child of God. Discern every *spirit.*

So in the practice of their craft they're listening to and summoning up demons that they think make them powerful and they think they can get these demons to do their bidding. But it's a trap, for humans. After a while, when these demons take over that so-called spiritualist, they're gonna need God for real.

The Take Over

The Book of the Revelation records a letter to the Church at Ephesus, the church that worships the moon *goddess,* And this is what the letter said to the Angel of the Church in Ephesus. I write:

Verse 4: Yet I hold this against you. You have forsaken the love. You had it first. Consider how far you have fallen. Repent and do the things you did at first if you do not repent. That will come to you and remove your lampstand from its place. But you have this in your favor. You hate the practices of the Nicolaitans, which I also hate. Whoever has ears to hear, let him hear what the Spirit says to the churches. To the one who is victorious. I will give the right to eat from the tree of life. Which is in the paradise of God.

God's first Commandment and probably number one pet peeve is **idolatry**. Swearing to, praying to, incanting to, worshipping the moon or whatever entity you think lives there, knowingly or unknowingly is still idolatry.

Do Not Swear by the Moon, actually, don't swear by anything but keep your oaths and vows made to God.

I personally have noticed that people are really *different* on a full moon. They're erratic or weird. When I see unusual or erratic behavior, especially at night, I've asked people for years, *Is it a full moon?* According to some sources, the full moon doesn't even really affect anybody, except maybe people who have bipolar disorder.

I say it affects pretty much everybody, unless you are really prayed up. Evil is enchanting all the more on a full moon, so we might see people acting all kinds of *different* on the full moon without even realizing they're being *different* at all.

Occultic, and satanic organizations learn about the *Triangular Powers,* while basic people, even Christians learn a few facts about ocean tides, the distance the moon is from the Earth, and the size of the moon in six grade science, then we leave it there.

No, we need to learn what they know, too. Ocean tides are **feet** higher on a full moon and when the gravitational pull of the moon causes a high tide, on one side of the Earth, there's a high tide on the other side as well. Water levels are up. *Majini*? Water Kingdom?

People are affected by the full moon, because the moon worshippers, the enchanters and those who practice dark arts are out there, heightening their activities at night and especially at full moons.

So, if we are in war, and we are, and the enemy has weapons that we can plainly see with our eyes open, and he's using them against us, wouldn't it be wise for us to learn about those weapons, and how they work? I'm not even talking about the weapons we don't even know about yet, and that's another whole book. But the sun is a weapon. Uh-huh. The Moon is a weapon? Uh huh. If evil can take something big, powerful, and in plain sight and use it as a weapon, we should learn about that.

I found this limerick online, about the moon:

The man in the moon came to me.

He was tall, as I could see.

He then looked so feared he magically disappeared. ..

Then the rest of the limerick—the writer, Maggie's Blog says that they were now scared for all eternity.

You may notice there are some words I don't use, some phrases I don't speak, that's me. You do what's right for you. And I definitely won't write negative things for all posterity. Nope. I won't do it. I seek to devil-proof my words, whether spoken, thought, or written.

FYI: an evil **thought** needs to be countered with a Godly word **spoken** over it. Do not just do a mental erasure of an evil thought. Chances are good that it wasn't even your thought anyway. The devil is constantly trying to feed us, influence thoughts, ideas, to promote his program.

Don't even *say* things that can be taken out of context and misused against you.

Seems excessive? It's not. Whenever he can, the devil will misuse your words to entrap you, if it is at all possible. The only way the devil is not paying any attention to you is if he already has you.

You need to devil proof your words.

It could be that moon limerick is a time lapsed snapshot of what will eventually become of those who chant into the moon.

Between the beginning and the end of that limerick a lot of devastation against the children of God may happen if we're not prayed up. But, if that Christian prays and is prayed up, eventually what the enchanter desired to happen to a person will happen to the one enchanting evil spells, and curses.

People, I am calling you to your prayer closets. Get to praying.

The Saved Life

Where is your spiritual covering, anyway? And what's the difference between your life and the life of your unsaved neighbor? Anything?

I'm asking you for your real life. I'm asking you for right now, not just your afterlife. What is the difference between your life and the life of your unsaved neighbor?

If you've been affected or indoctrinated by any of what is in this book, there are fire prayers at the back of this book.

Whether you are worker in the dark arts or the innocent who played Ouija Board, 8 Ball, or other "childhood" games, went to a palmist at the beach or dabbled online or in some way, you've got to renounce all these sins, including witchcraft, divination, tarot, crystals, horoscopes, astrology, numerology, Angel numbers, New Age--, all that stuff.

You can't mix and match with God. When you read your Bible, God will tell you clearly what you can do, what you cannot do, what He finds unsavory, and even abominable.

Those who work evil using the sun and the moon are wicked people. They're determined and they're proud of their powers.

I'm admonishing all slack Christians to command your day; you need to command the night. You need to command the sun and the moon, the Earth--, everything. Because people will use any part of the universe to enchant curses and spells against others, especially against Christians.

As a Christian, you cannot afford to miss your prayers. You cannot afford **not** to be prayed up 24/7. To the *It-don't-take-all-that crowd*, it does take all that.

Christians, stop standing around stunned when something happens. Command the night, command the day. Be proactive, be progressive.

And if you know that someone is programming celestial bodies to the harm of mankind, especially Christians and especially you and your family, you have authority to do something about it. Do something about it.

I'm Not Enchanted to Meet You

Enchanters are working with *familiar spirits*. They've sized you up already from various *spirits* running in families. They've been assigned to you since your birth. They know everything about you. They know the chinks in your armor. They know your points of weakness. They know what you are likely to do, and what you are likely not to do.

They tell this evil human agent who's working with them the best way, the best day, and the best time to attack you. Stay prayed up. Because we have the greater one in us, God will protect us. When this person who wants to attack you, checks for you and they find out that you're in God, Spirit-filled, you are a workman who studies and shows yourself approved, you are a prayer warrior, you're not slack with the things of God, they may keep on stepping, but even if they don't, the hedge of fire, the protection, the Blood of Jesus, the Fire of the Holy Ghost, will be strong, and they cannot penetrate that. The Name of the Lord is a strong tower. The righteous run in and they are safe. Hallelujah.

Witchcraft that is woven into the *Triangular Powers* can suddenly make people sick, fail, defeated, depressed--, any a number of evil things. *Went to bed last night fine, woke up this morning sick as a dog.* **WHAT** happened overnight?

The enemy happened.

Are you still frustrated by being hindered by problems every day? Stuff that should be simple, is problematic for you. If it is not because you are prayerless, look at *Triangular Powers*.

Are you going through ridiculous stuff? When I was much younger and carefree, I remember often going through so much ridiculous stuff because I was either praying wrong, praying weak prayers of unbelief, or distracted by my social life -- not praying at all.

So much weird stuff was happening to me that people thought I was making up the crazy mishaps in my life. But now that I know a bit more, thank You, Jesus, I see there was evil programming. Was it *triangular*? I don't know. Was it generational? Probably, yes. Maybe both. Maybe a combination. I just know it was hindering me and I had to do so much more to accomplish things that other people seemed to just be able to accomplish easily.

For example, I went through an entire first and second semester of college – that's a year. The following year, as a sophomore I had to go to Registration because for some reason, they didn't think I was an American citizen. That took months to clear up, although they had all my birth and other records since the year before.

I mean STUPID stuff! In my case it most often was paperwork. It's better now because I PRAY and command my days and nights and weeks, and months, and year!

Recommended book: **Time Is Of the Essence** by this author.

So we learn here that evil programming is in the *powers above*, if the *triangular powers* are being invoked against the Earth, against the inhabitants, especially against Christians.

Warrior Angels

God has warrior angels because He needs them. There is warfare being invoked by evil workers if *Triangular Powers* are being used against the Earth or Her inhabitants. To answer that, when we pray and when we speak the Word of God, we can deploy God's warrior angels.

Those who believe that nothing is going on, won't do anything. They won't fight, they will not possess their possessions, they will not get the things that belong to their peace and their salvation. But you need to fight. And that calls for the whole armor of God, all the spiritual weapons and warfare, prayer, fasting, and watching.

Command the day. Command the night so that you are speaking to those celestial powers that evil has found a way to *triangulate*.

Evil Enchanters will enchant, hours and hours against the object of their hatred, they are dedicated. I'm not trying to give anybody a persecution complex, but Evil hates Christians. Period. Evil human agents who are full of hate will chant specifically against certain *someones*, but they also enchant against cities, territories, regions, states, and countries. They are on their evil assignments and must do as they are told.

It is our duty as Christians, as sons of God-, yes, we want to save our own hide, but we must also pray for our church, neighborhood, and community.

Evil is not stronger than good. We can't let evil dedication be stronger than Christian dedication. Evil Enchanters are up in the night all night, chanting and muttering spells and enchantments against their would-be victims, perhaps programming the sun or the moon, or the sun and the moon, the stars, and other celestial bodies.

Moon enchantments can be especially dangerous because the *good* Christians are at home asleep. As you know when you're asleep, you have no idea what's going on around you.

Moon enchantments can catch a man when he's *really* unawares because he is asleep.

Sun enchantments are programmed into the sun which means the *timing* of the sun, when the sun rises, every time the sun rises, at the *time* the sun rises, perhaps one curse is programmed to afflict you either once at that time daily for a certain amount of time, forever, or cyclically, with *each* rising of the sun until you are consumed.

Those who send affliction to you don't plan to afflict you just once. Those who send death spells to you are serious and plan to see it through. According to Pius Joseph, if you are afflicted in any organ of your body that is essential for life, a death spell has been sent to you. https://a.co/d/ba6SD0d

If you aren't serious, get serious.

The sun shines in the daytime, of course, but you can't *see* charms; they are spiritually discerned. If you are one to pray diligently and pay very close attention to your dreams, ask God, *What are you showing me here?*

Oh, the Greater One is in us, but witchcraft is very powerful, if unopposed. That is, if we're not doing anything about it to counter it. We can't do anything much about it If we're both naturally **and spiritually** *asleep*.

Some people put themselves chemically **and** pharmaceutically asleep. They're drunk, drugged up. If you don't have any idea what's going on in your real life. You could be an easy victim.

Remember, even if your pastor is praying for you, he's not praying *instead* of you. You need to be praying for yourself.

God is Sovereign, God is strong, and mighty, He is able, but we are assigned in the Earth right now, set in Dominion with authority. We are supposed to be like God; so in the Earth we should be strong and mighty and doing exploits as instructed by Jesus. Repeating, Heaven and Earth must agree; some things cannot even happen in the Earth until we **agree** with God.

The Enchanters are agreeing with the evil in the 2nd Heaven so that evil can come to Earth. They may be up all night doing that, or they may get up at midnight, the Witching hour. From midnight to 6:00 AM is a very dangerous time for Christians because we're asleep. Of course, depending on what time zone they live in, their spell casting may be during your daytime hours. Unless the Lord tells you or the witch brags, you may not ever know who is enchanting against you.

We need rest and balance to maintain our health, but we also need prayers. If you're a day bird and you married a night bird, that may be good so there will be prayer coverage in your house, if you're a praying family. I hope you are.

Proclaim you this among the Gentiles. Prepare war. Wake up the mighty men of war. (Joel 3:9)

Are you dedicated to being Christian, doing what Christians do, or do you want to punch the *I-went-to-church time clock* and just learn *stuff* just to know it?

Resist the devil and he'll flee from you.

(James 4:7)

Don't ignore the devil; he is real. He exists and he is evil. This is one time where denial doesn't work. Because the angels come for our words (Daniel 10:12). we need to keep talking, keep praying, keep praying, keep praying because most of the world, and carnal folks are agreeing with the 2nd heaven, and there's the answer to the question, *Why does it seem that the world is so evil?* Or is there more evil in the world than there used to be?

On one hand, whatever a person agrees with from the heavenlies, that thing is given permission to come to Earth in general, and specifically, come to your life.

On the other hand, if you're **not** agreeing with evil, but you're also NOT disagreeing with it and evil human agents are at work directing evil at their target of jealousy or hatred--, it could land. If you're the target and you're in a dry season, not being prayed up, *tag*, you're it.

Today.

I say today, because eventually that evil power that they have summoned will also turn on and torment the person who is summoning them or do even worse to them. If in that time, you have started prevailing prayers, the evil may not continue against you, but it may have turned back on them. If you have not started praying, the evil may be on you *and* them. It depends.

Christians, Sons of God, we need to agree with the 3rd Heaven where God lives. *Let it be done on Earth as it is in Heaven.* **God has empowered us to <u>agree</u> with Him to bring godly things into the Earth** such as more mercy, more grace, more favor, provision, and protection from heavenly realms to Earth. That's what we are here for, to let it be done on Earth as it is in Heaven, to make Earth look more like the 3rd Heaven. **In essence, we have authority to accept or reject what should be coming to Earth.**

Evil agents are **misusing** their *human* authority to both invite and accept delivery of evil onto the planet and direct it into the lives of unsuspecting folks. There are about a million of them right now, whereas Christians are supposed to be 210 million strong in the USA. It is easy to ask, Why is there so much evil? Why is there so much stealing, killing, destroying in this country, right now? Christians, what are you doing? What are you *agreeing* with?

Simplifying that, if there is one evil person for every 210 good people, **why is there so much evil?** One sinner can destroy much good, but <u>one</u> evil person opposed to 210 good people--, come on Christians, what are we doing?

At 200 to 1, we should have already whipped the devil and all evil in this country.

The Four One-One

The Lord shared with me just this morning that the Bible has been in print, and available for mass readership for the past 411 years. That's about, what--, 10 generations? Shouldn't we know what's in it by now and be asking God **what *else* do we need to know?** Instead of having to go back and be taught all over again and again and again, generation after generation.

Four hundred and eleven years--, 411 years 411, shouldn't we have the 411 (the four-one-one) on the devil by now?

We can't be ignorant. We have to know our authority in the Lord and *use* it. Our full authority. You may have prayed, and nothing seemed to have happened. Keep praying. The *Triangular Powers* may have been invoked to work against your state, your city, your town, your neighborhood, your community, your street, and/or you in particular.

Even if **you** get your breakthrough, if your neighborhood, community, your territory has legal, evil, unopposed coverage, that can still hinder *your* blessings. We walk in Dominion championing over territorial, neighborhood, community, city, state principalities, as we have authority. Do not overstep authority when praying, but we have authority over *Triangular Powers*. Use every authority that God has given into your hands.

Christians need to be the people who know how to work with the *Triangular Powers* for good. We need to advance our warfare or at least defend it when the evil human agents invoke *Triangular Powers* to put their desires into effect.

God made creation to serve us, and we need to **work it.** We need to work it. We need to work that authority. Speak, decree, declare, pray. The Greater One is in us so we can't let that one sinner do a lot of damage. If we say we are Christians and there are 210 of us to oppose <u>one</u> sinner to stop evil from coming to the Earth, let's do it. Amen.

For Our Words

The Angels of God come for our words; we must give voice to the Word of God to assist our Angels in their works on our behalf; this is called praying. We pray all kinds of prayers including spiritual warfare, decreeing and declaring. We must pray our Angels *through*.

We have to pray our Angels **through** the second heaven which is a region of heavy warfare and entanglements. Satan does not want us to talk to God, interact with God, hear from God, receive from God. But we must; it is how we live.

There is evil in heavenly places; that is the warfare. The Angels come for our words to fulfill our requests to God for our country, state, city or neighborhood, for ourselves, and our fellow man. We can't leave Angels hanging in the second heaven in warfare by just praying a little and then not praying anymore.

Anyone who has ever been on a missions trip can tell you that even though they went to minister to others, to help others, that they themselves ended up being changed, and changed for the better. So, when you are praying for your community, neighborhood and country, you are praying against powers that your neighbor may also be praying against, even though he's in his own home and you're in yours. There are territorial powers that affect territories, and in praying for *others*, you are praying broader, far-reaching prayers that help others, as well as yourself.

Always pray; pray for yourself, and for others.

Warfare & Deliverance Prayers

Father, in the Name of Jesus, anything in me that is blocking the heavenlies from fighting for me, I repent, now. I repent for every sin that I have committed against You and Your Word. Lord, please forgive me.

I repent for my ancestors' sins going back 10 generations on each side of my family, I am repenting for all their sins and their indiscretions, their evil oaths, their evil vows, loyalty and blood, oaths to Freemasons, Eastern Star, Shriners, Prince Hall Lodge, and any other secret society such as fraternities and sororities.

I repent for and I renounce every secret oath, and vow, forced or willing, in the Name of Jesus. Lord, cover them with the Blood of Jesus.

Father, forgive. Jesus please impute Your righteousness to me, thank You, Lord.

Lord, I repent for sins committed by anyone from my bloodline, anyone who has recited vows and oaths required to join the Masonic Lodge, any fraternity, sorority or any other secret society. I ask forgiveness for the sins of pledging allegiance to any foreign or false *god by any name*, in Jesus' Name.

Blood of Jesus, cover these sins and wash me clean, in the Name of Jesus.

Lord, break the curses and deliver me from the consequences of these curses.

As a result of these thousand oaths, these masonic oaths--, Lord, I renounce the oaths spoken and break the curses involved in any masonic order or degree in the Name of Jesus, please break the effect on the throat, the tongue.

I renounce the hoodwink, the blindfold and its effects on the emotions, eyes, including fear, confusion, fear of the dark, fear of the light, fear of sudden noises.

I renounce all tattoos, branding, markings of any kind, in the Name of Jesus.

I renounce all secret words, passwords, and code words. I renounce secret gestures, dances, steps, handshakes. I renounce the mixing truth and error, mixing truth and lies, in the Name of Jesus.

I renounce the noose around the neck, the fear of choking, every kind of hazing, and every *spirit* causing symptoms and diseases including, asthma, hay fever, emphysema, and any other breathing difficulties.

I renounce the compass point, sword or spear held against the breast, the fear of death by stabbing, the fear of heart attack, in the Name of, and through the Blood of Jesus Christ. Lord, we now pray for healing of the throat, vocal cords, nasal passages, sinus, bronchial tubes, lungs, and for healing, and the speech area and release of the Word of God to me, and through me for my family, in the Name of Jesus.

I command all demons assigned to enforce the curse or curses to leave now. Since the renunciation, you no longer have any legal right to stay, in the Name of Jesus.

I petition You, Lord, to remove the scales off my eyes and understanding, off me and anyone else ensnared by this enemy.

Lord, may others come to know the truth of the secret societies that approach them, or that they are interested in, so they and their family bloodlines do not get trapped in them, in the Name of Jesus.

Lord, set me free from every region of captivity, where I've been ensnared by my own doing, by ancestral curse or evil foundation, in the Name of Jesus. I renounce and break every secret society curse, in the Name of Jesus.

Lord, forgive my ignorance, I thought I was doing a good thing. Lord, forgive my ancestors, they may not have known that the secret society would not provide for them, but that it would take away from their lives and be a curse into their generations.

I command every demon working this curse to leave now, in the Name of Jesus, the Lord rebuke you.

I renounce polytheism, serving the idol *gods* of false religions, secret societies, college frats/ sororities. I renounce, oaths, vows and commitments to idol *gods* of the sun, and of the moon or any other celestial body, in the Name of Jesus.

I renounce all evil covenants I've agreed to, either knowingly or unknowingly. Lord, I break every curse on my life. I bind every enforcing demon, in the Name of Jesus.

Anything in me that is blocking Heaven from fighting for me or blocking the Lord from hearing and answering my prayer, come out, come up and out, in the Name of Jesus. Lord, I receive your deliverance now. Amen.

Idol *gods* of Roman, Greek, Egyptian and other mythologies that I've either knowingly or unknowingly declared oaths to, I break those covenants now and command every demon and evil *spirit* hired to enforce the curses associated with serving idol *gods* to leave my presence and leave my life now, in the Name of Jesus. Lord, forgive me, and remove the iniquity associated with this idolatry, which You hate.

Every soul tie and covenant that has legalized my captivity, I break it now, I break it, now I break it, in the Name of Jesus.

Lord, arise and contend with those who contend with me, in Jesus' Name.

All demonic interference with Angels of God, I bind you, the Lord Jesus rebuke you now in Jesus' Name.

By Thunder, by Fire, I break up every evil altar erected against me, in the Name of Jesus.

Every curse, every covenant, every soul tie--, break now! (X3), in the Name of Jesus.

I break free from the yoke and the covenant and shackles of every *Triangular Power,* in the Name of Jesus.

Ancestral dedication of my life to idols or occultic powers, I break you now, and I cancel you by Holy Ghost Fire, in the Name of Jesus.

Spirit of retaliation, *I bind you in the* Name of Jesus. You will not have an open door for return for pay back, in the Name of Jesus.

Lord, by Your mighty angels, seal up every dimensional access point to my life, in the Name of Jesus. Seal up access to me in every realm, age, timeline and dimension, in Jesus' Name.

(Pray this only if you mean it.) **Lord, wake me up, get me up when it's time to pray. Fill me with the *Spirit of Prayer* that I pray all kinds of**

prayers and I am effective in the Spirit, in the Name of Jesus.

Lord, if anyone is enchanting against me, wake me up if I'm sleeping, get me up if I'm resting, stir me up if I'm idle, and fire me up by the Holy Spirit, in the Name of Jesus, Amen.

Every evil power using *Triangular Power*s to attack me, I bind you, I paralyze you. Die! in the Name of Jesus.

I disconnect my life from all evil that employs *Triangular Powers,* in the Name of Jesus. Every evil arrow from the sun, the moon, and stars release me; back to sender.

Every power trying to swallow my prayers, I command you to choke, retch, and vomit out my prayers and all communications to and from the 3rd Heaven. My prayers are none of your business. I bind you from interfering again. I deafen your ears; I blind your eyes from hearing and seeing what I am saying to or hearing from My Father, when I'm speaking to my Father, and not to you, in the Name of Jesus.

I command you to forget what you saw. Forget what you heard regarding, me, my life or anyone in my family or under my stewardship.

I take authority over the effects of the elements, especially the *Triangular Powers*, the sun, the moon, and the stars, I command the day and the night, I bind them to the will of God in my life, in the Name of Jesus.

Earth and womb of the Earth you will not work against me, forever. Hear the Word of the Lord, and obey God and God's words, never the words of my enemies, in the Name of Jesus.

Earth & Time, wherever God has commanded the blessing for me, **Time,** work in my favor, so I am in the right place, at the right time always, in the Name of Jesus.

I command all the elements of creation to hear and obey. As the day breaks, Earth get in position to shake the wickedness from the four corners of the Earth, and yield provision and increase to me, in the Name of Jesus.

Sun, you will not smite me. Moon, you will not smite me, you will not obey the voice of my enemies, in the Name of Jesus.

I cancel, by Fire, every evil incantation against me, in Jesus' Name. Lord let their wickedness either correct them or condemn them. Lord, You know.

I prophesy the will of God, at every dawn: tender mercies. Thank You, Lord.

Thank You, Lord, for Your Grace, Mercy, and lovingkindness, in the Name of Jesus.

Moon, I declare you were created to glorify God and to light the night for the children of God. I command all evil, triangulating through the moon against me to cease, in the Name of Jesus.

I command the night: Moon and stars, you will not afflict me by night.

I destroy all evil programming made by my enemies into the Moon, stars, skies, heavenlies, any planet, Galaxy, Solar System, asteroid, Comet, meteor, any celestial body, the entire universe.

I bind any attack upon my life at night. Let the evening tide trouble the enemies that attack my life at night, in the Name of Jesus.

I bind and rebuke every *evil spirit* that walks at night. I bind and rebuke the pestilence that walks in darkness. I rest at night because I dwell in safety and the Lord gives me sleep.

God gives His angels charge over me to keep me in all my ways. Angels of God keep watch over me, and protect me so that I do not even dash my foot on a stone, so that I do not slip, fall or fail, in the Name of Jesus.

Lord, You will hear my prayers in the night watches. Thank You for hearing my prayers and answering, great is Your faithfulness.

I bind the rebuke every vampiric, marine, incubus, succubus *spirits* including Lilith and every *spirit of vexation* that would attack at night, in the Name of Jesus.

I bind and take authority over all nightmares, demonic dreams, nightmares, night terrors and masquerades, in the dream, in the Name of Jesus.

Every demonic dream sent into the night, into the sleep, whether I remember those dreams or not, I bring you all under the Blood of Jesus and I cancel you all. I declare you will have no effect on me, and you will fall to the ground as nothing, in the Name of Jesus.

My spirit, my spirit man, arise, be strong, hear the Word of the Lord and perform it in the dream. My soul, rest, my flesh, stand down – my spirit man is running the night, while you both rest, in the Name of Jesus.

I break every evil agreement made in the dream, in the Name of Jesus.

All assignments made against me in the dream are broken and will fall to the ground and disintegrate like dust and sand now, in the Name of Jesus.

Locusts of God, devour all evil imparted into me in the night, all injections, insertions, implants of every kind are now consumed and brought to nothing, by the Holy Fire of God.

I renounce and break the power of all evil altars and evil sacrifices made against me, in the Name of Jesus, and I declare they will have no impact on me.

All evil *spirit* food, and counterfeit gifts are rejected; I vomit it out, I return all gifts, in the Name of Jesus.

The Blood of Jesus covers me, my house, my family, and everything under my stewardship.

Thank You, Lord for this new day that You have made. I will rejoice and be glad in it, in the Name of Jesus.

Every enchanter, witch, or wizard working against me, either on your own behalf or by proxy, *triangulating* with or enchanting into any moon, the full moon, half moon, crescent, gibbous, Blue Moon, Pink Moon, Strawberry Moon, Harvest Moon, Libra Moon, Taurus moon–, any moon, lose your power and lose your connections, in the Name of Jesus.

Every enchanter, witch, or wizard working against me, either on your own behalf or by proxy, **forget my name, lose my coordinates, lose my location,** in the Name of Jesus. I smoke bomb your covens, and send you confusion from the war room of God.

Household practitioners of the black arts, I bind you from attending any more coven meetings, in the Name of Jesus. I bind you. I bind you; I block you; I block you, I put up obstacles in the spirit to keep you from joining your coven, ever again, in the Name of Jesus.

Territorial practitioners of the black arts, I bind you from attending any more coven meetings, in the Name of Jesus. I bind you. I bind you; I block you, I block you, I put up obstacles in the spirit to keep you from joining your coven, ever again, in the Name of Jesus.

Environmental practitioners of the black arts, I bind you from attending any more coven meetings, in the Name of Jesus. I bind you. I bind you; I block you; I block you, I put up obstacles in the spirit to keep you from joining your coven, ever again, in the Name of Jesus.

Heavens, praise the Lord for which you were created. Refuse to conduct warfare against my life, in the Name of Jesus.

Every evil programmed into my bloodline from the sun you are cancelled right now, in the Name of Jesus.

Every evil programmed into my bloodline from the moon be cancelled right now, in the Name of Jesus.

Stars, you fought against Sisera, you will now fight FOR me, not against me, in the Name of Jesus.

Sun and moon, every evil and incantation, hex, vex, spell intended for me, see this Shield of Faith? Ricochet. Go back to sender, in the Name of Jesus.

Blood of Jesus, wipe away every evil handwriting that is in the sun, moon, or the heavenlies against me, in the Name of Jesus.

I command the *Triangular Powers*, the *Powers Above*, to fight *for* me, not against me, in the Name of Jesus.

Sun, obey the voice of the Word of God. Do not smite me by day, not this day, or any day, in the Name of Jesus.

Moon, obey the voice of the words of God. Do not smite me by night, not this night, or any night, in the Name of Jesus.

Lord, raise an overpowering and ferocious adversary against the enemies of my destiny, in the Name of Jesus.

Lord, send every threatening power back to the abyss from where there is no return, in the Name of Jesus.

Every evil person, entity, or power that is working against my life, my health, my success, my marriage and family, Lord Jesus, cut off their power from the powers of all the elements, in the Name of Jesus.

Every evil person, entity, or power that is working against my street, neighborhood, town, city, state or country – this whole Earth, Lord Jesus, cut off their power from the powers of all the elements, in the Name of Jesus.

Cut off their power from the powers of the Sun, the moon, and the stars. Shut off their connection from the powers of all the waters, the seas, oceans, rivers, any water, in Jesus' Name.

Disconnect them from the powers of the Earth's soil, stones, trees--, and the network of all other witchcraft spirits. Cut them off. Cut them off by Fire, in the Name of Jesus.

The powers of the wind and the sky, the powers of fire—Lord, sever their connections, in the Name of Jesus.

Father, stop all *Triangular Powers* from working against me, in the Name of Jesus.

Every evil incantation uttered into the sun, Moon, stars, water, Earth, wind, fire, any pot, charm, or against, against me, be nullified by the Blood of Jesus.

I cancel all Satanic decrees and desires against my life, by the power in the Blood of Jesus Christ, in the Name of Jesus.

Every witchcraft kitchen, cooking up evil food for me, eat it yourself, and then you and your kitchen catch fire and burn all the way down, in the Name of Jesus.

Any power seeking to devour my increases, Holy Ghost Fire make them fall into the abyss from where they cannot return, in the Name of Jesus.

Every altar against me incorporating the sun, moon, o stars, for evil programming, lose your calendar, lose your clock and timer against me, and roast to ashes, by Fire and brimstone right now, in the Name of Jesus.

Fire of God, I call Fire, Fire of God against every evil altar erected or working against me or my bloodline, in the Name of Jesus.

Hailstones of God break up every altar to complete annihilation, in the Name of Jesus.

Fire. Fire, I call down Fire of God. Lord put a hedge of Fire, a wall of Fire, a mountain of Fire around me; make me too hot for my enemies to come close to me, in Jesus' Name.

My life, receive Fire, be charged with Fire become Holy Ghost Fire so that no evil and no demon can touch, in the Name of Jesus.

Charms that get their strength from evil heavenly powers, I command you to lose all potency against me, in the Name of Jesus. Return to sender.

Every evil programmed into the moon against my relationships, the Lord Jesus deny you access to me by Fire, in the Name of Jesus.

I command the night and the day. I command the sun and the moon and the stars: you will not afflict me, but you will work in my favor, for my goodness, for my success, for my blessings and prosperity, in business, in life, in relationships and family, in the Name of Jesus. Thank You, Lord. I count this as done, in the mighty Name of Jesus. Amen.

Jesus, I invite you into my life, my household. Lord, expose every household enemy, in the Name of Jesus.

Thank You for the Wisdom, and authority and power to deal with this, and to deal with the moon.

Oh God, arise as a man of war which You are, and disgrace openly all the enemies of my destiny, all the enemies that don't want me to arise and shine, in the Name of Jesus.

I command Fire from the 3rd Heaven to locate all my spiritual blessings in the Heavenlies and consume all that are assigned to delay my blessings, in Jesus Name.

Any plantation in me that is not of God come out by Fire. Any darkness in me, come out by the Light of the World.

Evil timetables, evil timelines, evil handwriting, evil scrolls, every handwriting against me, *triangulated* with the moon, receive the razor of God, and be shredded and then burnt to ashes, in the Name of Jesus.

Every battle against my calling and ministry in the Heavenlies, hear the Word of the Lord, and scatter by Thunder, in Jesus' Name.

Every satanic power assigned to shut my heavens for favor in the heavenlies die, in the Name of Jesus.

All that rightfully belongs to me in the heavenlies be released to me by Fire, in the Name of Jesus.

Long-awaited blessings that belong to me, that have been hijacked by the powers in the second heavens, be released by Fire, now, in the Name of Jesus.

Thank You, Lord. Thank You, Lord, for your Salvation and deliverance from the evil trap of moon worship, in the Name of Jesus,

Lord, restore the years the locusts have eaten. Restore the years of the palmer worm and the caterpillar have taken from me personally, and from my family, in the Name of Jesus.

Lord, please release the blessing of healing on me and my family, in the Name of Jesus.

Lord, remove this *little g god* and his influence from our lives forever, in the Name of Jesus.

Father, thank You, Jesus. You are the Light of the World. You are my Salvation and You are my Peace. You are the Truth. You're the Only Living God, and I thank You, Lord, I bless You. Thank You and I bless You, in the Name of Jesus.

Amen.

Prayerbooks by this author

While most books by this author have prayer points either throughout the book or at the end, there are some books that are only prayers. You just open up the book and pray. They are listed below:

Prayers Against Barrenness: *For Success in Business and Life*

Fruit of the Womb: *Prayers Against Barrenness*

Beauty Curses, *Warfare Prayers Against*
https://a.co/d/5Xlc20M

Courts of Marriage: Prayers for Marriage in the Courts of Heaven *(prayerbook)* https://a.co/d/cNAdgAq

Courtroom Warfare @ Midnight *(prayerbook)*
https://a.co/d/5fc7Qdp

Demonic Cobwebs *(prayerbook)* https://a.co/d/fp9Oa2H

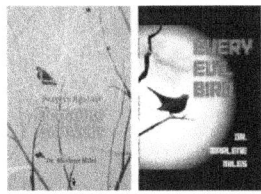

Every Evil Bird https://a.co/d/hF1kh1O

Gates of Thanksgiving

Spirits of Death, Hell & the Grave, Pass Over Me and My House

Throne of Grace: Courtroom Prayer

Warfare Prayer Against Poverty
https://a.co/d/bZ61lYu

Other books by this author

AK: The Adventures of the Agape Kid

Already Married in the Spirit: *Why You May Not Be Married in the Natural*

AMONG SOME THIEVES

Ancestral Powers

Anti-Marriage, *The Spirit of*

Backstabbers https://a.co/d/gi8iBxf

Barrenness, *Prayers Against* https://a.co/d/feUltIs

Battlefield of Marriage, *The*

Beware of the Dog: Prayers Against Dogs in the Dream.

Bless Your Food: *Let the Dining Table be Undefiled*

Blindsided: *Has the Old Man Bewitched You?* https://a.co/d/5O2fLLR

Break Free from Collective Captivity

Broken Spirits & Dry Bones

Casting Down Imaginations

Churchzilla, The Wanna-Be, Supposed-to-be Bride of Christ

Demonic Cobwebs (prayerbook)

Demonic Time Bombs

Demons Hate Questions

Devil Loves Trauma, *The*

Devil Weapons: Unforgiveness, Bitterness,…

The Devourers: Thieves of Darkness 2

Do Not Swear by the Moon

Don't Refuse Me, Lord (4 book series)

https://a.co/d/idP34LG

Dream Defilement

The Emptiers: *Thieves of Darkness, 1*
https://a.co/d/5I4n5mc

Evil Touch

Failed Assignment

Fantasy Spirit Spouse https://a.co/d/hW7oYbX

FAT Demons (The): *Breaking Demonic Curses*
https://a.co/d/4kP8wV1

The Fold (5-book series)

- The Fold (Book 1)
- Name Your Seed (Book 2)
- The Poor Attitudes of Money (3)
- Do Not Orphan Your Seed (4)
- For the Sake of the Gospel (5)
- My Sowing Journal

Gang Ups: Touch Not God's Anointed

Getting Rid of Evil Spiritual Food

https://a.co/d/i2L3WYQ

got HEALING? Verses for Life

got LOVE? Verses for Life

got HOPE? Verses for Life

got money? https://a.co/d/g2av41N

How to Dental Assist

How to Dental Assist2: Be Productive, Not Wasteful

How to STOP Being a Blind Witch or Warlock

I Take It Back

Legacy

Let Me Have A Dollar's Worth
https://a.co/d/h8F8XgE

Level the Playing Field

Living for the NOW of God

Lose My Location https://a.co/d/crD6mV9

Love Breaks Your Heart

Made Perfect In Love

Man Safari, *The*

Marriage Ed. Rules of Engagement & Marriage

Made Perfect in Love

Money Hunters: Beware of Those

Money on the Altar https://a.co/d/4EqJ2Nr

Mulberry Tree, *The* https://a.co/d/9nR9rRb

Motherboard (The) - *Soul Prosperity Series*

Name Your Seed

Occupy: *Until I Return*

Plantation Souls

Players Gonna Play

Power Money: Nine Times the Tithe

https://a.co/d/gRt41gy

The Power of Wealth *(forthcoming)*

Powers Above

The Robe, Part 1, The Lessons of Joseph

The Robe, Part II, The Lessons of Joseph

Seasons of Grief

Seasons of Waiting

Seasons of War

Second Marriage, Third--, *Any Marriage*

https://a.co/d/6m6GN4N

Sift You Like Wheat

Six Men Short: What Has Happened to all the Men?

Soul Prosperity soul prosperity series 3

https://a.co/d/5p8YvCN

Souls Captivity soul prosperity series 2

The Spirit of Anti-Marriage

The Spirit of Poverty

StarStruck

SUNBLOCK

The Swallowers: *Thieves of Darkness*, 3

Take It Back

This Is NOT That: How to Keep Demons from Coming at You

Time Is of the Essence

Too Many Wives: *Why You Have Lady Problems*

Tormenting Spirits   https://a.co/d/dAogEJf

Toxic Souls

Triangular Power *(series)*

- Powers Above

- SUNBLOCK
- Do Not Swear by the Moon
- STARSTRUCK

Unbreak My Heart: *Don't Let Me Die*

Uncontested Doom

Unguarded Hours, *The*

Unseen Life, *The* (forthcoming)

Upgrade: How to Get Out of Survival Mode

- Toxic Souls (Book 2 of series)
- Legacy (Book 3 of series)

The Wasters: *Thieves of Darkness,* Bk 2
https://a.co/d/bUvI9Jo

What Have You to Declare? What Do You Have With You from Where You've Been?

When I Was A Child, *I Prayed As a Child*

When the Devourer is Rebuked

https://a.co/d/1HVv8oq

The Wilderness Romance *(series)* This series is about conducting a Godly relationship and marriage with someone who is a Wilderness person. It is about how to recognize it and navigate through it. These books are about how not to get caught up in such.

- *The Social Wilderness*
- *The Sexual Wilderness*

- *The Spiritual Wilderness*

Other Series

The Fold (a series on Godly finances)
https://a.co/d/4hz3unj

Soul Prosperity Series https://a.co/d/bz2M42q

Spirit Spouse books

https://a.co/d/9VehDSo

https://a.co/d/97sKOwm

Battlefield of Marriage, The

https://a.co/d/eUDzizO

Players Gonna Play

https://a.co/d/2hzGw3N

Matters of the Heart

Made Perfect in Love https://a.co/d/70MQW3O

Love Breaks Your Heart https://a.co/d/4KvuQLZ

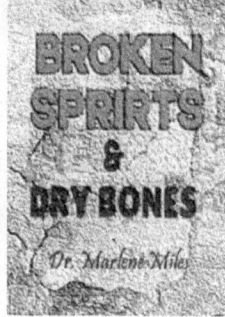

Unbreak My Heart https://a.co/d/84ceZ6M

Broken Spirits & Dry Bones https://a.co/d/e6iedNP

Thieves of Darkness series

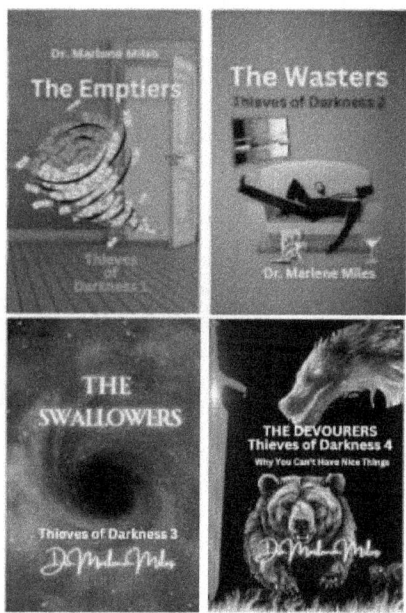

The Emptiers https://a.co/d/heio0dO

The Wasters https://a.co/d/5TG1iNQ

The Swallowers https://a.co/d/1jWhM6G

The Devourers: Why We Can't Have Nice Things
https://a.co/d/87Tejbf

Triangular Powers https://a.co/d/aUCjAWC

Upgrade (series) *How to Get Out of Survival Mode*
https://a.co/d/aTERhX0

But I tell you not to swear at all, either by heaven or it is God's thrown, or by the earth, for it is his footstool, or by Jerusalem, for this the city of the Great King. (Matthew 5:33-34).

What are the Triangular Powers and are they hindering your breakthroughs?
Book 3 of the Series

Dr. Marlene Miles has served in Ministry 20+ years, she holds two Doctorate Degrees in Ministry. She writes for both adult Christians and children.

Freshwater Press
ISBN: 978-1-960150-41-7
eBook Version

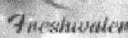
Freshwater

www.ingramcontent.com/pod-product-compliance
Lightning Source LLC
Chambersburg PA
CBHW070855050426
42453CB00012B/2215